# MARK CULLEN
## THE COMPLETE GARDENER

# FURNISHINGS

**Ballantine Books**

Ballantine Books
A division of Random House of Canada Limited
1265 Aerowood Drive
Mississauga, ON  L4W 1B9

INFACT Publishing Ltd.
66 Portland St., 2nd Floor
Toronto, ON  M5V 2M8

CTV Television Network Ltd.
250 Yonge St., 18th Floor
Toronto, ON  M5B 2N8

**Canadian Cataloguing in Publication Data**

Cullen, Mark, 1956—
        Furnishings
(Mark Cullen's Complete gardener series)
Accompanied by video.
Includes index.
ISBN 0-345-39829-7

1. Garden ornaments and furniture.  I. Title. II. Series: Cullen, Mark, 1956— .  Mark Cullen's Complete gardener series.

SB473.5.C85 1996    645'.8    C96-930031-X

PHOTOS: Janet Davis—p. 6,9,10,17,24,27,29, 31, 37, 40, 47, 50, 61, 66, 69, 75, 79, 90; Ted Johnston-p. 45
SENIOR EDITOR: Wendy Thomas
HORTICULTURAL EDITOR: Denis Flanagan
COPY EDITOR: Sylvia Gilchrist
CTV CO-ORDINATOR: Glen Dickout, Manager, Special Projects
PROJECT MANAGER: Susan Yates, INFACT Publishing
COVER AND TEXT DESIGN AND ILLUSTRATION ART: ArtPlus: Brant Cowie, Dave Murphy and Jerry Stapley
SPECIAL THANKS: Dan Matheson, Canada am; Jean and John Farintosh; Aunt Charlotte and Uncle Tom; Len Cullen, my Dad; and especially, Mary for her help and support.

M+M Communications, Unionville, ON is the publishing imprint of Mary and Mark Cullen.

Printed and bound in Canada by Metropole Litho Inc.

# TABLE OF CONTENTS

· · · · · · · · · · · · · · · · · · · · · · · · · · · · · · ·

# INTRODUCTION

"What exactly do you do?" I am sometimes asked, in reference to my "day job." My response to that is to suggest that my professional goal in life is to remove the hocus-pocus, or the barriers, that Canadians imagine stand between them and success in the garden.

This book and video are a natural extension of what I do with great passion every day. My intent is to show you how to get the most out of your garden and to do it by minimizing the "work" (maintenance) and maximizing what I believe to be the most pleasurable aspects of gardening, including lounging around the yard in a favourite chair or hammock.

My good friend Dan Matheson is no gardening dummy. Truth is, he is a fast learner with more enthusiasm than most of us can imagine. He also has a habit of asking the very questions that Canadian gardeners (and non gardeners!) have on their minds at the time. I think you will enjoy this book and video as we simplify gardening and help you to get the most from your Canadian garden through *The Complete Gardener.*

Gardens are meant for your enjoyment and the enjoyment of your family and visitors. This means you need a place to sit, to play, to walk, to relax as you delight in the beauty you've created. But furnishing a garden goes beyond tables and chairs — this volume is full of ideas for adding interest to your outdoor room. I hope you enjoy this book as you consider furnishings for your garden.

MARK CULLEN

# FURNISHINGS FOR PLANTS

●●●●●●●●●●●●●●●●●●●●●●●●●●●●●●●●

T he containers in which plants are grown can serve two purposes: to provide a home for plants and to be decorative. Used alone or as an adjunct to beds, containers provide the gardener with great versatility. They can be used to change colour schemes, to retire spent plants, and to give plants the conditions they need in which to grow. Container growing is a popular form of gardening, especially for those who garden in confined areas or for whom kneeling and cultivating a garden is difficult. There are many types of containers which you can use in your garden.

## FLOWER POTS

Most flower pots — pots in which a single specimen is grown — are pretty utilitarian. The pots show off plants to great advantage by not competing with their colourful contents. Arranged in a group, potted plants can make a stunning display at the edge of a swimming pool, at the corner of a deck, or marching up steps. They can be re-arranged to provide different colour and plant combinations.

*Flower pots grouped together like this make a stunning display.*

Going beyond the strictly utilitarian, though, it is not hard to find flower pots in attractive shapes and designs that fit in with the theme of your garden. Architectural shapes look best with a modern, classical or formal style of garden; whereas more ornate pots are shown off to best advantage in a romantic garden. Rustic finishes or designs are appropriate for a cottage garden.

Here are some hints about choosing flower pots and caring for them:

❋ Unglazed terra cotta or red clay pots will dry out quickly but they are also more stable than plastic pots in windy weather. It is also easy to see when plants in a clay pot need watering — the pots become lighter in colour.

❋ Plastic pots will hold water longer than clay ones.

❀ Plants in containers need watering frequently. Over-watering is usually not a problem in pots, but they must contain drainage holes.

❀ At season's end, potting soil and spent plants can be put in the compost. Clean all pots before storing them. For winter care of plants in larger pots, see the next section on planters and urns.

## Suggested plantings of annuals for pots

Alyssum (**s**)

Coleus (**s**)

Geraniums (**s**)

Grasses (**s/sh**)

Herbs (such as parsley, chives, basil, mint, thyme, sage) (**s**)

Impatiens (**sh**)

Ivy (**sh**)

Lobelia (**s**)

Nasturtiums (**s**)

Nicotiana (**s**)

Pansies  (**sh/s**)

Petunias (**s**)

Sedums (**s**)

Succulents (**s**)

Verbena (**s**)

**s** = sun, **sh** = shade

# PLANTERS AND URNS

The difference between a pot, a planter, and an urn is a bit arbitrary. I tend to think of planters as being large pots that can take several plants. Items that can be used as planters are unlimited. If it can hold soil, it's a planter! Tubs, half barrels, baskets, sinks, troughs and old work boots are only a few of the containers you can use. As with other garden accessories, match the type of container to the mood or theme of your garden. Urns can be rather formal, although there are designs and patterns that can make them appropriate for gardens with a more casual mood. They frequently sit on a pedestal and may have decorative handles. Urns are attractive on their own and can be used simply as unplanted ornamental additions to the garden.

Containers are constructed from a wide variety of materials — wood, metal, fibreglass, terra cotta, and ceramic are common. Planters made from redwood, cedar, or teak are rot-resistant, although lining any wooden planter with a plastic liner (which can be made from a garbage bag), will extend its life. Just be sure to always puncture the bottom of the bag to make drainage holes.

Let's look at some of the advantages and disadvantages of the various materials.

❋

**TERRA COTTA:** Advantages: inexpensive; attractive; porous (allows roots to breathe); available in a variety of shapes and sizes. Disadvantages: easily chipped or broken; soil dries out quickly; can be heavy to move; cannot be left outside full of soil in most Canadian winters.

❋

**METAL:** Advantages: can be lightweight; warms up quickly in spring. Disadvantages: can rust; overheats in hot weather.

❋

**PRESSED FIBRE,** such as cocoa and paper fibre: Advantages: lightweight; attractive colour. Disadvantages: soil dries out quickly; material is not long-lasting.

❋

**WOOD:** Advantages: good permanent containers; easy to build; provides good insulation to roots; allows air into roots; can be painted various colours or stained; can be left out in winter. Disadvantage: can be heavy, especially when wet.

❋

**CONCRETE:** Advantages: available in a wide range of styles; can be left outdoors in winter, though some protection is advisable. Disadvantage: heavy, poor quality concrete can crack, splinter, and peel over time.

❁ ........................................................................

**PLASTIC:** Advantages: inexpensive; lightweight; holds moisture longer than terra cotta; long life; easy to clean. Disadvantages: can be knocked over by strong winds.

❁ ........................................................................

**FIBREGLASS:** Advantages: durable; attractive; lightweight; easy to clean. Disadvantages: expensive; may fade with exposure to sun.

## RULE OF THUMB:

All containers should have drainage holes.

*An urn is an attention-getter in any setting to show off flowers and to make a focal point.*

## OTHER CONTAINERS

❉ Another type of container is a jardinière. This is usually a decorative ceramic or stoneware jar that is used to display house plants or other plants. The potted plant is set in the jardinière, sometimes on a bed of pebbles to allow excess water to have a place to go and to prevent the plant from sitting in water. Potted bog plants can be set directly in a jardinière with a bit of water as they like to have their roots in water. Jardinières are available in a wide range of shapes, sizes, and colours.

❉ Strawberry pots are tall cylindrical-shaped red clay pots with little openings into which small plants can be put. The top is open and can be planted as well. In spite of the name, plants other than strawberries can be grown in them. Herbs and sedums do especially well, as the soil tends to dry out quickly.

At the end of the growing season, planters in which annuals have been grown can be emptied into the compost. Planters that contain perennials should be treated as follows:

❉ Snip off spent plant material.

❉ If the container is portable, store it in a shed, unheated basement, sun porch, greenhouse, or garage.

*Columbine is an often-used, beautiful perennial. It provides a tall accent for an urn or other planter.*

❀

If the container is too large to be moved, cover the soil with branches or mulch with straw for winter protection. To protect the plants and planters from strong winds, wrap them in burlap. If possible, move the planter to a sheltered spot for the winter, perhaps in the corner of a patio or deck.

❀

Gardeners who live in the milder regions of Canada, where winter temperatures don't drop below –5°C, can leave many containers outside throughout the year.

A small vegetable garden can also be grown in pots, so don't confine yourself to just flowers. Tomatoes and leaf lettuce do especially well in pots. Leaf lettuce doesn't need too much sun, but tomatoes crave it. Pots allow you to move these vegetables around during the day to give them the conditions they prefer.

## Suggested plantings for planters and urns

ANNUALS
The plants listed under Suggested plantings of annuals for pots, p. 7, as well as:

Balcon geraniums (**s**)
Candytuft (**s**)
Daisies (**s**)
Fibrous begonia (**s/sh**)
German ivy (**s**)
Hanging begonia (**sh**)
Impatiens (**sh**)
Marigolds, dwarf (**s**)
Morning glory, with
    support (**s**)
Multiflora petunias (**s**)
Salvia, dwarf (**s**)

Snapdragon, dwarf (**s**)
Stock (**s**)
Sweet pea, with support (**s**)
Trailing Lobelia (**s**)

PERENNIALS
Astilbe (**s**)
Columbine (**s**)
Coral bells (**s/sh**)
Ferns (**sh**)
Hosta(**sh**)
Iris (**s**)
Primula (**s**)
Rosemary (**s**)
Sage (**s**)

**s** = sun, **sh** = shade

*Hanging baskets of flowers need lots of care—watering, dead-heading and fertilizing. But they repay your attention magnificently!*

## HANGING BASKETS

Hanging baskets are popular, and for many they have become a traditional Mother's Day gift — that tells you how special they can be. Anybody can plant a hanging basket with colourful annual flowering plants, but not everyone is willing to maintain them.

Hanging baskets are intensive-care plantings. The city of Victoria in British Columbia is famous for its hanging baskets, but a small army of municipal workers keeps them at their height of perfection all summer long. For many of us our hanging basket by midsummer is a sad-looking reminder of our dreams. However, properly maintained hanging baskets add colour and character to any outdoor living area. Choose your hanging basket by the level of care you are willing to lavish on its plants.

Hanging baskets come in two forms that I describe as open and solid.

## OPEN HANGING BASKETS

The open form is made of wire or plastic strips fashioned in a bowl shape. Unmilled sphagnum moss or cocoa fibre is used as a liner to hold the soil. Plants are inserted between the ribs so that their roots penetrate through the moss or fibre into the planting soil. The top of the basket is also planted. Some garden centres sell hanging baskets that have the sphagnum moss already in place.

Preformed liners made of pressed cocoa fibre that fit into a plastic open basket are an alternative to the sphagnum moss, although it doesn't allow plants to be inserted in the sides of the basket.

## SOLID HANGING BASKETS

Solid baskets are made of plastic or wood, often with an attached saucer that acts as a moisture reservoir. The advantage is that these baskets don't need watering as frequently as the open type, but they are not as attractive and don't allow plants to be inserted on the sides. However, cascades of lobelia, petunias, and ivy geraniums will soon obscure the plastic as they mature.

## END-OF-SEASON CARE

At the end of the season, empty your hanging baskets and put the soil and plants on the compost.

Clean plastic baskets before storing in a shed or garage. The sphagnum moss used in open hanging baskets can be saved for use next year.

## Suggested plantings for hanging baskets

Begonias (**sh**)

Browallia (**s**)

Fibrous begonias (**s/sh**)

Fuchsia (**sh**)

Hanging begonias (**sh**)

Ivy geraniums (Balcon type are my favourites!) (**s**/part **sh**)

Lobelia (**s**)

Monkey flower (**s**)

Nasturtiums (**s**)

Petunias (**s**)

Portulaca (**s**)

Thunbergia (black-eyed Susan vine) (**s**)

Vinca (**s/sh**)

**s** = sun, **sh** = shade

---

### RULE OF THUMB:

Look for "multiflora petunias" when you buy annual bedding plants for best performance in containers. Petunias are not what they used to be! They have been improved upon over recent years and will now flower constantly all summer long if you give them a weekly feeding of 20-20-20 and a severe cutting back (by half) during the first week of August.

---

## WINDOW BOXES

On a busy city street, I love to look up and see an exuberant and lavish bunch of flowers tumbling out of a window box. It delights me to see the tried-and-true favourite petunias — but don't stop at petunias. Even though they are now available in a wider range of colours and forms than ever before, petunias are only the beginning when you are planting window boxes. Why not try some other colourful favourites.

*Window boxes can be planted with flowers (top),
a combination of flowers and trailing plants (centre) or for
winter, evergreens and arranged boughs (bottom).
Any way you choose, they make an eye-catching display.*

In our modern houses and apartments, window sills are virtually non-existent but hardware has been made which allows us to continue using window boxes. This hardware has, fortunately, also opened up a wider use for these versatile containers. Decks, fences, and walls now can all be anchors for window boxes.

❄ Window boxes are made in wood, metal, plastic, fiberglass, cement, and terra cotta in a variety of widths and depths. The deeper the better, to prolong moisture retention. On the other hand, the lighter the box, the easier it is to mount.

❁

Window boxes need drainage holes, so you should take some care when you are deciding where to position them. You don't want to water someone who is underneath as well as the plants! If the box is tilted slightly forward, any water or soil that drips or falls out is less likely to stain the wall below.

❁

Consider exactly how you will reach your window boxes to water the plants. If they are difficult to reach, you are unlikely to keep up the important watering regimen (which can be daily in a sunny spot during the severe heat of mid-summer). Also, if your windows open outwards or have screens, window boxes are one garden feature you should live without.

❁

Window boxes should also be fitted with feet if they are to sit on a sill or other type of ledge. Like most containers, window boxes will dry out quickly and will need frequent watering, so you don't want the water to collect between the bottom of the box and the sill or ledge.

❁

Plastic window boxes are plentiful and inexpensive, but they are not always the most attractive. Plan your plantings with many of the trailing plants recommended for hanging baskets to quickly conceal the (usually) white plastic.

❁

It is important to firmly anchor your window box. Planter box brackets are available, but choose carefully. They must be sturdy and adjustable to accommodate various widths.

❁

In the winter, fill window boxes with evergreen boughs of pine, spruce, or yew. A few red branches such as dogwood make a nice addition.

## Suggested plantings for window boxes

All of the plants listed under Suggested plantings of annuals for pots, p. 7, and hanging baskets, p. 14, as well as:

Hardy bulbs like tulips, crocus, hyacinth, daffodils (**s**)
Miniature roses (**s**)
Poppies (**s**)
Primroses (**s/sh**)
Spring flowering Heliotrope (**s**)

**s** = sun, **sh** = shade

---

### RULE OF THUMB:

Water and 20-20-20 fertilizer are the two key ingredients to all successful container gardening. Water diligently, applying generous quantities when the soil surface is dry to the touch. Fertilize annuals and perennials every 7 to 10 days with water soluble 20-20-20. For perennials, fertilize from planting time until late July, and from planting time until mid-September for annuals.

*Most houses no longer have window sills to hold window boxes, so like this one, the window box must be firmly affixed to the wall of the house.*

## Making a "Stone" Trough

You are unlikely to find many original stone troughs anywhere in Canada. If any exist, they have probably been brought here from Europe. But you can make a trough that is lightweight, will withstand the rigours of our winters, and will provide a unique container for alpines, bonsai plants, and other small and sprawling plants.

### What You'll Need
- Plastic sheeting
- Two strong cardboard boxes, one larger than the other
- Strong tape (e.g. duct tape)
- Portland cement
- Perlite or vermiculite
- Dry sphagnum peat moss
- Concrete colouring powder (optional)
- Chicken wire, 1.2 cm (1/2-inch) mesh
- Dowelling, three pieces 1.2 cm (1/2 inch) in diameter
- Sharp knife
- Bucket
- Rubber gloves
- Empty tin
- Wire cutters
- Old knife

**To make the trough, you will need a space**
- where it doesn't matter if you make a bit of a mess;
- that doesn't have to be used for anything else for a few days; and
- is close to a water source.

### How to Make the Trough
1. The large box dictates the outside measurements of the trough. The small one should leave a gap

Start with two card-
board boxes; the
larger strengthened
with bands of duct-
type tape.

After pouring in
a layer of concrete,
fit in a piece of
chicken wire.

Cover the chicken
wire with more
cement and then
insert the dowels
to form future
drainage holes.

Once the smaller box is
positioned, the concrete
can be poured around.

of 4 cm to 5 cm (1.5 to 2 inches) on all sides when placed in the larger box. The large box should be at least 8 cm (3 inches) taller than the small one.If adjustments need to be made to the smaller box to make it fit inside the large one with the required gap, cut the cardboard and tape it firmly to make the proper dimensions.

With tape, reinforce the larger box horizontally around the sides to prevent it buckling from the force of the wet cement. Use the plastic sheeting to protect the surface you'll be working on.

2. Use two parts dry Portland cement, three parts sphagnum moss, three parts perlite or vermiculite.

3. Using the empty tin as a measuring cup, measure out the required proportions of moss and perlite. Perlite gives a finish that's rougher than vermiculite, and more stone-like. Add the colouring agent if you are using one — use 125 mL (1/2 cup) of the concrete colouring powder for every litre (quart) of cement — then add the cement. Work with fairly small portions at a time. This prevents a large batch hardening before you can use it all. It also means you won't make more than you will need.

4. Add water, mixing to the consistency of creamy cottage cheese.

5. Pour a layer, 2.5 cm (1 inch) deep, in the bottom of the large box. Cut the chicken wire to the size of the bottom of the box and insert the wire into the cement until the wire is covered.

6. Add another layer — again, 2.5 cm (1 inch) deep — of cement to completely cover the wire. Pack down to remove air bubbles.

7. Insert the dowels in the cement. They will form the drainage holes.

8. Insert the smaller box, open side down, into the larger box. Position it so that it is centred. Push it into the cement so that it will make a slight indentation.

9. Cut more chicken wire so that it will fit snugly in the space between the large and small boxes. It should be the same height as the small box.

10. Insert the strips of chicken wire in the space between the boxes. Press it firmly so that it sits in the cement at the bottom and leave it for about 30 minutes.

11. Mix more cement and pack it into the space between the two boxes. Make sure the wire is covered. Tap or shake the box gently to get rid of air bubbles.

12. Let the cement cure for three days, then remove the large box. Spray the outside of the container lightly with water, then leave for another seven days. The more slowly the concrete hardens, the stronger and more durable the pot. Cover with plastic if you think it's drying out too quickly.

13. After seven days, remove the dowels and the small box, then leave for another seven days.
14. Let the container sit outdoors for six to eight weeks. If rain is infrequent during this time, water it now and then to leach out the lime contained by cement. The lime will be toxic to plants.

**Suggested plantings for the trough**

| | |
|---|---|
| Alyssum (**s**) | Primula (**s/sh**) |
| Arabis (**s**) | Rock pink (**s**) |
| Armeria (**s**) | Sedums, cacti and |
| Dwarf columbine (**s/sh**) | succulents (**s**) |
| Forget-me-not (**s/sh**) | |

**s** = sun, **sh** = shade

House plants such as baby's tears, creeping fig, polka-dot plant, grape ivy, English ivy (troughs planted with house plants would have to be moved in for the winter)

# FURNISHINGS FOR PEOPLE

· · · · · · · · · · · · · · · · · · · · · · · · · ·

**M**ost people who garden regularly don't consider gardening to be "work." I find it a relaxing way to forget the stresses of running a business but I have to admit that once the work is done, I like to sit in a comfortable chair and enjoy the way my garden looks, sounds, and even smells. The flowers, shrubs, and trees are lovely on their own, but a well-placed statue, sculpture, or other garden decoration offers an appealing view, as well.

## STATUARY AND DECORATIVE FIGURES

The choice of garden decorations has increased dramatically in the past few years and by poking around your local hardware store, checking out the garden centre, and attending craft fairs, you'll be exposed to a wide variety of these furnishings. Whether your tastes lean to a grouping of wooden hens and chickens strutting across your lawn or a classic Greek figure in flowing robes, it should not be hard for you to find the right accent.

The patron saint of gardening, by the way, is St. Fiacre. You can recognize him by the spade and small plant his is usually holding. A statue of him makes a great addition to any garden, no matter the style.

## USING STATUARY AND FIGURINES

Some gardeners dream of adding a finishing touch to their garden with a piece of classic statuary. Many of these pieces have come from Europe or are modelled on the classic European style. Figures in flowing robes, nymphs, cherubs, sea horses, and sea shells are some of the most common.

*Statues in the garden can be of the classic type, such as this, or of the modern variety.*

*It is important to match the theme of your garden to your statuary or figurines.*

Other gardeners tend to the more whimsical, using figurines in a variety of materials of animals, such as cows, pigs, or lambs, or even the ubiquitous pink flamingos.

The important thing is to know the style of garden you have planted and the decorations which will best support that style. Here are a few pointers to help you when you go shopping — or when you head for your workshop or studio to make your own.

✤ Statuary can provide a focal point, something the eye is drawn to immediately, or it can be a pleasant surprise — a frog peeping out from beneath a group of hostas or a rabbit half-hidden by ferns.

✤ Barnyard animals add a rural or pastoral touch to your garden. They look best in a country-style garden — one that has flowing lines, colourful beds, and a cheerful atmosphere. If you have twig or rustic garden furniture, a flock of sheep grazing on the grass will look right at home.

✤ Gnomes, cartoon characters, and flamingos should be used sparingly unless you are very sure of what you are doing. Placed strategically, flamingos can be used as a touch of humour in the garden. There is room for whimsical decorations in your garden if you are making the statement "This is a fun place to be!" — otherwise restraint is the key!

✤ A romantic garden, full of rampant lush roses, intertwining clematis, and scented lavender, is the perfect spot for a cherub or nymph. Don't overdo it. One small statue is more impressive than three or four.

✤ Gardens designed in a Japanese style benefit from the careful placing of stone Japanese lanterns, Buddhas, miniature pagodas, or temple guard dogs.

✸ Even in a small space, a figurine placed among containers can provide the finishing touch. Sometimes the container itself is also the piece of decoration — some containers are decorated with faces or other designs in bas-relief.

✸ Wrought iron sculptures can be particularly attractive in the winter. Not only do they stand out well against the snow, their lines are emphasized by a dusting of snow.

✸ Decorative materials don't have to be freestanding. You can find bas-relief gargoyles, lion's heads, and sun faces that are designed to be attached to walls or posts.

✸ A sculpture looks best positioned with a hedge, fence, or wall as a backdrop.

✸ If the sculpture seems overwhelmed by surrounding growth, place it on a pedestal set among bushes to show it to advantage. A sculpture placed just around a corner or in a place where the garden visitor unexpectedly comes upon it causes a pleasant surprise.

## CARING FOR STATUARY AND FIGURINES

Most figurines and statues will not need a lot of upkeep; in fact, many of them seem to improve with age as they survive the vagaries of our sometimes harsh Canadian climate. In winter, it's the freezing; in summer, it's the strong sun. These garden decorations come in a wide variety of materials but the most common are concrete, wood, metal, plastic, and terra cotta.

✸ Wood should be well-painted. Extend the life of wooden figurines by storing them in a shed or garage over the winter.

✸ Objects made of plastic or clay need to be stored in a sheltered spot over the winter. Plastics can crack and fade and porous clay will crack after several freezing and thawing cycles.

✴ ┄┄┄┄┄┄┄┄┄┄┄┄┄┄┄┄┄┄┄┄┄┄┄┄┄

Metals such as wrought iron should be checked each year for cracking and peeling paint and rust. Use a wire-bristled brush to get rid of rust and cracked paint, then paint with a good paint made for out-door use.

✴ ┄┄┄┄┄┄┄┄┄┄┄┄┄┄┄┄┄┄┄┄┄┄┄┄┄

If you are ever in doubt about the ability of your statuary to withstand winters, play it safe and shelter it. If the piece is heavy, it will have to be left outdoors — be sure to check with the person you bought it from as to its weather resistance.

## SUNDIALS

The sundial is more an ornamental addition to the garden than a practical one. To be truly practical — that is, to tell the time with a sundial — it needs to

*Sundials make a charming addition to the garden, even if they are not used as reliable timepieces!*

be set up and calibrated carefully and to your particular location. It is not surprising that we don't rely on them as timepieces but use them as interesting and pretty garden decorations. Nevertheless, they should be placed as if they were a functioning piece of equipment.

❋ The sundial is made up of two sections, the dial and the gnomon. The gnomon is the sloping piece that casts the shadow.

❋ If a sundial is to tell the time fairly accurately, the angle of the gnomon in relation to the horizon should be the same as the latitude of the place where it is set up. You can usually adjust the gnomon on mass-produced sundials to correct the angle, if necessary. At noon, the shadow of the gnomon will fall directly below it if it is set up properly.

❋ Place the sundial in a spot where it will be in sun for most of the day. Situate it so that the face can be looked down on easily.

❋ The dial and gnomon are often decorated with appropriate symbols or quotations, often related to the passing of time.

❋ The materials used for sundials are metal (often brass or bronze), stone or slate, although modern ones can be rendered in more modern materials such as heavy plastic.

❋ Some sundials can be attached to the wall, but many are freestanding so a base must be supplied.

❋ A sundial looks especially attractive at the centre of a knot garden or similar symmetrical planting. A sundial by a door can be nicely set off with a grouping of potted plants at its base.

# GAZING GLOBES

Gazing globe, witch's ball, reflective ball, mirror ball, lawn ball — call it what you will, it's an unusual addition to the garden decor. Unlike most of the other garden furnishings this has no purpose that I know of other than to be a wonderful attention getter! Its reflective qualities, however, will make a small garden appear larger.

* Globes range in size from 20 cm to 35 cm (8 to 14 inches) and are made of a mirror-like glass. They can sit on a pedestal or lie directly on the ground. They look best among flowers so that they can reflect the lively colours.

* They are made of glass, so don't place them near a play area. If they're under a tree, bring them in if a strong wind threatens — you don't want branches crashing down on them.

* Slightly irregular finishes indicate that the globe has been hand-blown. Moulded globes, which have seams, are less expensive.

* Gazing globes or simple glass balls floating in a water garden add a pretty dimension among water-lilies and reeds.

*Gazing globes, also known as witch's balls or mirror balls, are very popular right now. They are both unusual—and very pretty.*

# BENCHES, CHAIRS, TABLES, AND UMBRELLAS

When you buy garden furniture, especially benches and chairs, the most important consideration is the purpose of the piece. Is it meant for comfort or for decoration? It is possible to fulfil both requirements in one piece, of course, but there is a great deal of attractive garden furniture that just isn't nice to sit in. If comfort is important to you, sit in the chair or on the bench before you buy it. Is it easy to lower yourself and then get up again? Are there any bits that stick into you? Are the arms comfortable (and wide enough to hold a mug or book, if necessary)? Can the back be adjusted? If the piece doesn't measure up on the comfort scale but you love it anyway, there's no reason not to buy it — think of it as a piece of art.

Benches, chairs, and tables can be heavy and cumbersome to move and store. Look for materials such as teak that will withstand exposure to our harsh weather. Protecting wooden or metal furniture by painting or staining will help preserve them, but painting is a commitment — the furniture must be repainted regularly to prevent the furniture from becoming shabby looking. On the other hand, if you want to move furniture around — to take advantage of the sun's movement, for example — there are lots of easy-to-move tables and chairs available.

## BENCHES AND CHAIRS

The most basic piece of furniture in a garden should provide somewhere to sit — to rest from your labours, to admire the view, or to sit while you

*A twig bench suits the rustic or cottage garden. This is one type of furniture that can well withstand inclement weather!*

eat and drink. One of my earliest memories is that of Grandma Cullen's wraparound wrought iron bench at the back of the garden ringing an old pear tree. For purely practical purposes, an aluminum and webbing folding chair will fill the bill; but why not combine practicality with decorative appeal?

Whether your garden is a modern, formal, or cottage garden, there is a bench or chair to suit. All garden furniture should be able to withstand rain, but cushions should be waterproof or stored in a sheltered spot between uses. If you're short on storage space, look for furniture that can be folded or choose materials that can be left outdoors all year round. Look for metal decorations or fasteners on chairs in brass or galvanized metal as they won't rust.

❋ ...........................................................................................

Twig furniture suits the rustic cottage garden. Colourful chintz cushions can be brought outdoors as needed to make sitting more comfortable or to protect clothing. To extend the longevity of this furniture, store it inside during the winter. Twig furniture can be a way of you really interacting with your garden. There are several books and courses available to teach you how to construct twig furniture.

* * * * * * * * * * * * * *

Wicker and cane furniture is a lasting favourite and fibreglass or plastic furniture that's a dead ringer for wicker has the added advantage of being easy to clean. Painting real wicker furniture will help prolong its life and winter protection is desirable.

* * * * * * * * * * * * * *

Stone benches can be cold and hard to sit on but in the right setting, especially a romantic garden, they'll be right at home.

* * * * * * * * * * * * * *

Wood blends in well with other garden furnishings and plantings and is comfortable to sit on. Many woods, especially teak, weather well and require little maintenance. Softwoods, such as pine, need to be treated with a preservative annually. Seats should slope slightly or the seats should be slatted in some way to allow water to drain quickly. Most wooden furniture, especially if it's treated with preservatives, can be left out all year, giving some interest to the winter garden. Wood can also be used for built-in furniture that links various areas of the garden or provides a transition from one area to the next.

* * * * * * * * * * * * * *

Lutyens-style benches are quite elegant. They are so impressive that a Lutyens (pronounced Loo-chens) bench can become the focal point of a garden. Set against a backdrop of an ivied wall, they are shown off to perfection. They are made of wood and have rather high arms and a decorative back.

* * * * * * * * * * * * * *

Wrought iron furniture is suited to a romantic or formal garden. Depending on the design of the seat and back, wrought iron chairs and benches may not always be comfortable, but they can look fabulous with a

*A Lutyens bench is an investment for the garden. Their impressive elegance often sets them off as a focal point.*

matching table. Wrought iron demands some upkeep. Wash them and check for rusty spots every spring. Use a paint formulated for wrought iron to patch or repaint entirely. To prolong their life, store them in a protected place during the winter, although you can leave them out without severe damage. They also look attractive in the winter garden, especially if they're painted in a colour that shows well against the snow.

Reproduction cast-iron furniture is available from garden centres and manufacturers specializing in reproducing furniture, light stands, and brackets from the Victorian period. Often the arms and legs are made of cast iron or aluminum and the seat and backs are wood. Treat and store as you would wrought iron or wooden furniture.

Moulded resin never rusts or yellows. Most often, resin chairs are stackable so they are easy to put away for the winter. The designs are limited pretty much to a contemporary look, so they won't fit well into such gardens as the English country or Japanese. For a garden that fulfils a number of functions — dining room, play room, relaxation area — they're the ticket.

When buying inexpensive tubular aluminum furniture, which is rustproof, look for these construction details that indicate good quality: welded joints rather than screwed-together joints; "powder-coat" finish (which is electrostatically applied) rather than a sprayed-on finish.

❋

Deck chairs, made of wood and canvas, add a relaxed holiday feel to a garden. The canvas may need to be replaced every few years but many fabric shops sell striped or solid-coloured canvas for replacements. Keep the wood in good repair and waterproof by painting it every year. Store in a dry place over the winter. In regions with heavy rainfalls, it's best to store deck chairs in a dry spot when they are not in use.

❋

Adirondack or Muskoka chairs made of wood are popular. They have a feeling of cottage and small-town life about them and would be out of place in formal gardens. They often have wide arms which are useful for drinks or putting down your book while you wander off to dead-head something that's just caught your eye. Some people find the chairs difficult to get out of as they are rather low to the ground — others would see that as a good reason to stay put! Keep them painted or stained to protect from the weather and store in a dry place over the winter.

❋

If raised beds are part of your garden, incorporate seating around them to better enjoy the plants, especially the smaller ones.

❋

Benches, especially when they're either on the deck or part of a deck, can be incorporated with planters. It is not difficult to make your own, if you are so inclined, or to purchase a set at a garden centre or hardware store.

❋

A wooden tree seat can be the answer to a barren spot under a tree. It can be a simple ring around the tree or designed to be more ornate with a decorative back. Leave enough space for the trunk to expand if the tree is not fully grown. The ground should be made level some distance out from the circular bench so that the sitter's feet can reach the ground. Don't put a tree seat under trees that drop sticky residues or that bear fruits, such as mulberries, that stain.

Benches aren't just for sitting. Try putting a single potted plant on one end of a bench.

To paint or not to paint? Some wooden furniture weathers to a lovely grey and looks more natural in the garden if left that way. If the purpose of the furniture is to use it as a decoration, however, painting it will help draw attention to it.

A formal symmetrical bench is nicely set off by container plantings on each side. A twig bench or wicker seat looks best with a casual grouping of pots at one end.

## TABLES AND UMBRELLAS

Eating al fresco — outdoors, in other words — is one of the nicest things about summer. Food seems to taste better in the fresh air. When it has been cooked on a nearby barbecue, that's even better. Most people want a table outdoors for this purpose, but tables have other uses, too. They can also be used as work tables for garden chores or as a place to display potted plants.

Inexpensive, easy-care, utilitarian garden furniture is not hard to find. Table, chair, and umbrella sets are readily available at garden centres and hardware stores. They are often made of strong plastic, which wipes clean easily. The umbrellas come in a wide array of colours and patterns. Keep the umbrellas closed in windy weather and hose them off with a strong jet of water every now and then to dislodge bits of leaves and twigs that can cause them to discolour. To prolong their life, store the set in a dry place for the winter; although if space is at a premium, they can be left outdoors covered by a plastic tarp.

❋ Whether you are buying a set of table and chairs or tables and chairs that aren't a set but will be used as one, check to be sure the table is comfortable to eat from when you are sitting in the chair.

❋ Wooden tables and picnic benches need more upkeep than the plastic variety but often fit into the garden decor more naturally and can reflect the theme of the garden. Ornate iron legs topped with marble or other stone give a very different feel than a twig or wicker table. Solid wood table tops will not allow water to drain away quickly, so look for tables with slatted tops or small spaces between the lengths of wood. Wooden tables can be painted, stained, or left to weather naturally, although without some protective coating, their life will be shorter. Because wooden tables can be heavy and cumbersome, plan on leaving them outdoors over the winter. If possible, move them to a sheltered area or cover with a plastic tarp.

❋ Umbrellas can be purchased freestanding or as part of a set of table and chairs. The freestanding type, of course, offers more flexibility as it can be moved around the garden to provide protection as needed. Synthetic materials are usually inexpensive but will fade over the years. Canvas makes a beautiful, although expensive, umbrella that will need more care than the synthetic fabrics. A covered vent allows gusty breezes to escape so the umbrella won't topple. The fabric canopy should be scrubbed with a mild fabric detergent. Rinse well after soaping then leave open to dry. Umbrellas should never be closed when they are wet or damp as mildew will weaken the fibres. Some manufacturers will even make umbrellas from material you supply.

# MATCHING GARDEN FURNITURE TO THE MONOCHROMATIC GARDEN

When you have put hours of thought into the design of a monochromatic garden — one in which one colour predominates — you will want to complement the plantings with the colour of your garden furniture.

## THE BLUE GARDEN

Pure blues and purple-blues in the same garden need to be separated by other plants with grey or green foliage or white or bright-coloured flowers. Accent plantings of yellow, orange, or scarlet will provide a touch of liveliness. Woodwork painted green, white, or yellow will fit well into the scheme.

## THE GREY AND LAVENDER GARDEN

Grey and lavender give a restful feel to the garden. Don't confine yourself to flowers, though. Plants with grey foliage can be used to great advantage. Pale yellow and pale pink flowers are attractive additions and fit in well. Stone walls look lovely with this colour scheme, as does silver-grey furniture.

*A grey garden, such as this, is restful and has a calming effect. Silver-grey furniture best suits this colour scheme.*

## THE PINK GARDEN

Pinks must be carefully chosen as they can clash, but the movement from one type of pink to the next can be bridged nicely with grey foliage and plants with white flowers. Pale yellow and lavender are useful foils for pink. Furniture, fences, arbours, gates, seats, and so forth will be most effective if they are painted silver-grey, pure white, or a deep blue.

## THE RED GARDEN

An entirely red garden would be quite overwhelming, but it can be softened by the use of white and blue-grey flowers. Dark red and maroon judiciously used can help to tone down scarlet colours. Furnishings look stunning in a bright white in such a garden.

## THE WHITE GARDEN

Probably the most famous white garden is the garden of Vita Sackville-West at Sissinghurst in England.

When you start to choose plants for your white garden, you will be amazed at the great variety white encompasses — many "white" flowers have veins and tracings of green, rose, mauve, or yellow. A white garden is relaxing and peaceful and is at its best at night. Dark evergreens and plants with grey foliage show off white flowers well. Furniture of varying green and grey colours will be right at home.

## THE YELLOW GARDEN

Soften the effect of bright yellow and orange by displaying plants against an evergreen hedge or white wall. If the colour needs more cooling down, some companion flower colours would be white, sky-blue, or deep purple. Furnishings look best in pure white, light or dark green, or grey-blue.

# ARBOURS, PERGOLAS, AND GAZEBOS

Arbours, pergolas, and gazebos are often used interchangeably to describe garden structures. However, I distinguish them as follows:

❋
:   An arbour is a covered place in which to sit or pass through from one section of your yard to another. It may be formed by trees or created by shrubs or vines growing over latticework.

❋
:   A pergola is an arbor formed by vines or shrubs growing over a trellis or latticework and creating a series of arches that cover a path.

❋
:   A gazebo is a small building that usually contains furniture.

All add a romantic luxurious touch to the garden, especially arbours and gazebos which bring to mind lazy afternoons while someone else does the work!

Building any of these structures in your garden is a bold undertaking. Careful planning is essential. As you assess your garden and its potential for an arbour, pergola, or gazebo, take the following into account:

- Scale: The finished size must be in keeping with the size of the garden
- Proportion: A pleasing design — the height must not be too high for the width
- Style: The design and plantings must continue the theme of your garden

## ARBOURS AND PERGOLAS

**ARBOURS**   I'm tempted to say that an arbour is anything that isn't a pergola or gazebo — that's

*Arbour or pergola?—either way, an absolutely
lovely and romantic addition to the garden.*

how flexible an arbour is! Virtually any little nook
or cranny in the garden can be turned into an
arbour. Size and scale are not as vital a consideration as with a pergola or gazebo.

❋

An arbour can be used as a support for vines, but it
might not have any plants growing on it — somewhat like a more open gazebo. The design of such
arbours is important. The feeling or theme of the
garden should be reflected in the design as well as in
any furniture used in the arbour.

❋

Commercially made arbours are available, but check
them carefully to be sure their construction and
materials will be sturdy.

❋

Arbours are fairly easy for the home do-it-yourselfer to make. Wood is commonly used in the form of planks, sheets of trellis material, or rustic poles. Galvanized nails and bolts should be used to connect the various parts. Embed uprights in concrete for stability.

❋

An arbour that's little more than a covered "gateless gateway" provides a transition from one part of the garden to the other.

❋

Wrought iron arbours are usually quite delicate and the plantings should be correspondingly light and airy to allow the design to be seen and appreciated.

❋

Plantings to cover arbours are the same as for pergolas below, but use restraint if the arbour is in a small corner. Note that wisteria needs a good strong support on which to grow and silver-lace vine is attractive to bees.

**PERGOLA** Planning a pergola for the garden means you must face the fact that your garden probably is not a vast estate. Adding any kind of structure such as a pergola, arbour, or gazebo quickly brings home the importance of scale. Nevertheless, I have seen situations in which pergolas have been incorporated successfully in small gardens. Their presence was natural, well integrated, and not at all overwhelming. If you have a small garden, you might consider attending a local garden tour, often put on by horticultural societies, to see what others have done and what works and what doesn't. Many Canadian communities offer public access to otherwise private gardens for a day or two each season. The tours are inexpensive and your local horticultural society always welcomes visitors.

**Some uses for pergolas are:**
- To divide one section of the garden from another
- To lead to different sections of the garden
- To provide a covered walkway
- To shelter a patio or deck
- To frame a view or garden feature, such as a beautiful bench or impressive plant specimen
- To make a welcoming front entrance

To be successful, the pergola must have a purpose — that is, it must take the visitor somewhere or provide shelter. A pergola that has no purpose other than to act as a vehicle for vines or other plants is a forlorn and odd sight, it is better to build a simple trellis.

Here are some guidelines for planning, building, and planting the pergola.

❈

Ideally, a pergola should allow at least two to walk side by side, but many suburban and urban gardens would not allow such a generous width. With some clever planning and planting, however, a smaller scale pergola could become a mysterious and enticing feature. An arbour or pergola of only one or two sections can act as a "doorway" from one section of the small garden to the other. Don't forget that once the vines start to grow, the walkway will be smaller.

❈

Upright supports should be about 2 m (7 feet) apart and the same in height.

❈

Wooden poles make a rustic pergola. Other materials that can be used for the uprights are wooden beams; brick, stone, or cement columns; metal or steel pipes or columns. The uprights must be strong for they will support not only the crossbeams but the weight of the vines that will grow on the crossbeams.

Uprights should be well embedded in concrete so they can withstand strong winds.

The overhead crossbeams can be slender wood boards, stripped saplings, or lightweight metal poles. The heavier the vines are likely to be, the stronger the crossbeams should be.

Choose materials for construction that require little upkeep. When perennial vines start to cover the arbour or pergola, it will be difficult to paint.

The design of an arbour or pergola can be simple, just the uprights and crossbeams mentioned above. The feature of the arbour or pergola is the planting it supports. Look to gazebos for more decorative constructions. However, if you do choose a decorative pergola, keep the plantings fairly light so they don't overwhelm the underlying design.

A pergola looks best when smothered in vines. Depending on the size of your pergola use one or a combination of the following: wisteria, grapes,

*An arbour can be constructed in a formal fashion (left) or more casually, in a twig style (right).*

clematis, climbing roses, honeysuckle, Virginia creeper, or silver lace vine. The latter is a fast-growing dense climber. If you have room, plant vines that flower at different times — for example, a wisteria, which will flower in the spring, and an autumn-flowering clematis gives two seasons of interest to the pergola. Don't overburden a delicate-looking pergola — it might give the impression of imminent collapse even if the structure is well-built.

❄

The areas on either side of the pergola can be effectively planted as well. Shade-loving plants will do well, especially once the main plantings are mature. Anemones, primroses, violets, hostas, and forget-me-nots make pretty "foundation" plantings.

❄

It could prove difficult to grow grass in the walkway enclosed by the pergola because the walkway will be shaded when the vines reach maturity, Paving stones, brick, or gravel will make a good walking surface.

## GAZEBOS

In its rather dry fashion, the Concise Oxford Dictionary defines gazebo as a "structure whence a view may be had." In my 1936 Wm. H. Wise & Co. *Garden Encyclopedia* it is suggested that the gazebo was inspired by the watch tower in a medieval palace wall or battlement! Somehow these descriptions lack the romanticism that seems inherent in the word itself, and in the design of the building. Of all garden structures, the gazebo offers the best opportunity for fanciful creation. In today's garden it seems to be more the object to be viewed than to view from. However, whether it's meant as a focal point or a place from which to survey your garden, keep the style true to the style of your garden — a replica of a Japanese tea house

*A gazebo at water's edge is idyllic!*

is appropriate for a serene Japanese garden, and an airy latticed structure will fit into a romantic English cottage or country garden.

You must not get so carried away that you forget practicalities. Some kind of screening is a good addition if you intend to take meals in your gazebo. There is nothing romantic about spending mealtimes hiding food from flies and shooing wasps away. If the purpose of the gazebo is as a place to eat, don't site it so far away from the house that it becomes a chore getting the food there.

If the gazebo is to be used as a place of serenity and meditation, a place to read or relax, build in some comfortable benches or provide room for chairs or small sofas. Be sure that when you are seated, you can see out the openings or windows. Some gazebos are open on all sides, others are quite enclosed. Decide how protected from the elements you want to be.

Another use for a gazebo is as a potting shed. It should be constructed so that from the outside none of the associated odds and ends are visible — all watering cans, pots, flats, bags of potting soil, seed packets, and so forth should be out of sight.

## FOUNTAINS

One of the most peaceful and relaxing elements you can introduce into your garden is water. A small fountain can provide a soothing sound to mask out roaring traffic, noisy lawnmowers, and other intrusions.

It is surprising what a difference a small decorative fountain can make to the look and sound of your garden. The eye is drawn to water — whether the water is moving or still.

Adding a fountain to a garden or water garden is simple as long as there is an outdoor electrical outlet nearby. If you are having electrical power brought to the garden, hire a licensed electrician to do the job. Water and electricity are a potent and potentially fatal mix — you don't want to take chances. Specify that a circuit breaker is to be installed for safety's sake.

### RULE OF THUMB:

Tell a story. The non-plant features you add to your garden give greatest pleasure when they remind you of something or tell a story. For me, a small fountain fashioned after the artist's four-year old son holding a garden hose over his head did it. It took me years to find this gem, but to me it says columns about the most playful of all ages; and reminds me of my own son at that age.

# FREESTANDING FOUNTAINS

Freestanding fountains can be submerged in a water garden, be part of a garden feature such as a rock or millstone from which the water issues, or be part of a figurine or piece of statuary from which water flows into the water garden or other receptacle.

Fountain heads used in water gardens throw out various water patterns depending on their design. When you are purchasing equipment for the fountain, make sure your pump is powerful enough to produce the flow you need. Most home gardens are best served by fairly simple fountains so that their effect does not become overwhelming rather than relaxing. Incorporating a freestanding fountain in a formal or symmetrical design will look

*The sight and sound of water in a garden will draw the eye and relax the soul.*

better than using one in a more "natural" design that is an irregular shape and that attempts to look as if it is a natural part of your landscape. Keep in mind that if you want to grow water plants, too much turbulence caused by the fountain can damage them or prevent their flowering.

Some fountains are composed simply of the nozzle throwing up its pattern of water, but others are figures or statues holding jugs, bottles, or fish from which the water pours into the pool.

Another type of freestanding fountain, sometimes called a bubble fountain, is one that is not part of a water garden but is incorporated into a millstone or rock. Sometimes the feature is just a bed of river rock or attractive pebbles. The water bubbles out of an opening in the rock or centre of the millstone, spilling over it to a bed of river rock. The whole thing is set in a concealed reservoir, where the pump is housed, recirculating the water.

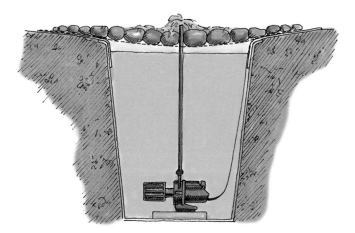

*A bubble fountain can be easily made with a garbage can, submersible pump, some chicken wire to hold the rocks, rocks for the water to trickle over and water!*

The fountain and its pump should sit on a stable base and be easily accessible so that the filter can be cleaned. Pumps can be either submersible or surface, but the former is most appropriate for home use. Surface pumps are used when a great volume of water needs to be circulated.

Pumps should not be left in ponds or pools over the winter so plan to dismantle the fountain in the fall and reassemble it each spring.

## MOUNTED FOUNTAINS

Wall fountains, or water spouts, are perfect for a small garden. They don't take up much space and are easy to dismantle for the winter. The range of such fountains is almost endless — a sculpture, mask, gargoyle, lion's head, sun face, and so forth. Found objects can sometimes be fashioned into a wall fountain with a little imagination and ingenuity. The water will trickle into a basin or other receptacle and be pumped back up through the wall to be recirculated.

These pieces of decoration are produced in various materials and can be left outside all winter if the material is weather-resistant. In the fall, drain all water and bring the pump indoors.

# WATER GARDENS

Many gardeners dream of having a water garden. If you're at the stage of turning the dream into reality, think of the uses of a water garden. Perhaps you want only a reflecting pond; maybe you want fish and water plants. What about including a fountain, as I've described above, or small waterfall? Then look at shapes. Many people like a pond to look natural and design it with curving edges; others opt for a more formal rectangle.

Choose the site for the pond carefully. If you want waterlilies or many of the other water plants, you will need a site that gets at least six hours of sun a day. Of course, sun means algae, but I will give you some hints on dealing with that later. If you want a pond for its reflecting qualities, you can choose a spot at the outer edge of a tree; the image of the leaves reflected in the water will be lovely, but you will also have to clean the pond more frequently.

---

**RULE OF THUMB:**

At least one third of the water surface in a water garden should be covered by plant growth.

If mosquitoes are breeding in your water garden, add a goldfish and they'll disappear.

---

*A water garden can be built in a large pot and planted with a few of the same plants that would go into a full-size water garden.*

## BUILDING THE WATER GARDEN

A properly installed and well-situated pond requires little upkeep. You will need a liner, either a rigid preformed basin or a sheet of flexible pond liner made of polyvinyl chloride (PVC). You can even buy a whole kit that contains everything you need for a water garden except the plants and fish.

To figure out the length of sheet you need, add the length of the pool to twice its depth and add 60 cm (2 feet); to figure out the width, add the width to twice the depth and add 60 cm (2 feet). Here's an example for a pond that's 1.2 m long (4 feet), 1.2 m wide (4 feet), and 45 cm (18 inches) deep:

(Metric calculation) 1.2 m + (2 x 45 cm) + 60 cm = 1.2 m + 90 cm + 60 cm = 2.7 m$^2$

(Imperial calculation) 4 feet + (2 x 18 inches) + 2 feet = 4 + 36 inches + 2 feet = 9 square feet.

Try to build your pond on a sunny day. Let the liner lie in the sun so that it will be flexible when it comes time to put it in the hole.

Mark out the shape of the pond with an old hose or a piece of rope. Move it around until you're happy with the shape. Then start digging following

the shape you have made with the hose or the shape of the preformed insert. If you want to have hardy waterlilies, a section of the pond should be at least 60 cm (2 feet) deep. The surrounding sections can be shallower, but at least 35 cm (14 inches), to accommodate other plants.

You will be backfilling the hole with sand, so dig it 7 cm to 10 cm (3 to 4 inches) deeper than the planned final depth. Once the hole is satisfactory, add a layer of sand at least 7 cm (3 inches) deep. This will protect the liner from any protruding roots or rocks.

Now spread the liner over the hole. Make sure that it covers the space evenly. If your pond has square corners, fold the material to make as neat a corner as possible. Once you are happy with it, use rocks, bricks, or other objects, light and not sharp, to secure it at the edges. Start filling it with water, smoothing and adjusting as the pond fills.

To make a neat edge, lift up the sod surrounding the pond and roll it back about 30 cm (1 foot). Slide the edge of the liner under the sod, then roll the sod over the liner. Cover the liner edge with brook stones, flagstones, or brick.

Before you add any plants or fish, let the pond sit for a couple of days to allow chemicals in the water to evaporate. You are likely to have a problem with algae in the beginning, even after you've done some planting, but don't rush to empty the pond and start all over again. It takes a while to reach balance in a new pond. Plants called oxygenators, such as water hyacinth, will help maintain the balance by competing with algae for nutrients. Algae need light to bloom, so allowing plants and their leaves to partially cover the surface of the pond will prevent excessive algae growth.

*This cross-section of a water garden shows how plants can be left in their pots for ease of removal at the end of the season.*

Wait for another two weeks before introducing fish to the pond. It is best not to overcrowd the fish in your pond. Plan on having one fish per 30 cm$^2$ (2 to 3 square feet) of water surface. Start with goldfish. Although koi are lovely to look at, they grow quite large and like to munch on the plant life in a pond, such as those waterlilies you've just planted.

When introducing the fish into the pond, leave the fish in the container you bought them in — usually a clear plastic bag. Put the container in the pool but do not open it. When it has reached the same temperature as the pool, open the bag and let the fish make their way out. If you have bought fish on a hot day, get them in the pond as quickly as possible; the water in the bag will warm up quickly on your way home and could cause the fish great distress, perhaps even death. Give the fish some food. At first they will seem shy and stay among the plants but in a few days they will seem quite at home.

Fish are quite sensitive to changes in their surroundings, especially water temperature, so do not add great amounts of cold water if the pond needs topping up. It's best to leave some water in a bucket, allowing the chemicals to escape and the water to take on the air temperature.

In the fall, be vigilant about keeping leaves out of the pool. Trim plants down to the surface of their container and put the material on the compost. Hardy waterlilies can be left in place, but tropicals need to go inside for the winter. Check with your supplier regarding other plants you purchased to see what kind of winter care they need.

It is not necessary to completely empty the pond every winter. In fact, once you have the balance established, it's advisable to leave it for as long as it continues to work well. If your pool is more than 90 cm (3 feet) deep, in most parts of the country your fish should survive the winter. They will stay in a state of hibernation until warm weather returns and do not need to be fed during the winter. On the other hand, to be entirely safe, bring them indoors for the winter, following the suggestions for introducing them to the pond — that is, allow them to be acclimatized and don't subject them to great changes in temperature.

You can leave the fish in place and be quite sure they will survive if you add a small water heater for the winter. An air pump keeps the water moving, provides oxygen, and lessens the chances of freezing. You can also lower the level of water after the first freezing by about 2.5 cm (1 inch). Melt a hole in the ice and siphon off some water. Let it refreeze, and then lower the level again. Air is trapped between the two layers and helps to insulate. Never strike the ice in an attempt to open it up. It will produce shock waves that will kill the fish.

Scavenger snails can help to maintain a clean pond.

# KIDS' PLAY AREAS

Kids and gardens sometimes don't get along very well. A kid might see your pride-of-joy perennial bed as the wall of a castle or a great place to hide from invaders from outer space. Don't despair — not only are there ways to accommodate your child's play needs with your desire to grow things, but you can plan for the future as your child outgrows sandboxes and swing sets.

If you are fortunate enough to have a large space, you will find it easy to accommodate a play area for your kids. Families with smaller spaces will have to be a bit more ingenious.

## RULE OF THUMB:

To encourage, motivate, and involve kids in gardens and gardening, think of yourself as a gardening coach and have only a few rules in the early stages.

## GENERAL CONSIDERATIONS

❋ Safety is the most important issue when it comes to children's play areas and equipment. Be sure the area is visible from the house.

❋ Incorporate some running space as children like space to run around in. However, this might not be possible in very small gardens and a sandbox or swing set may well be a better use of space.

❋ Inspect the play equipment frequently, checking for frayed ropes, protruding nails, bolts, or pegs, rough or sharp edges, and so forth. Look for footings that are exposed, cracked, or broken. Check for rot and signs of termites.

❋

Build or buy playground equipment that can be adjusted as the children grow. Most injuries that occur in a playground are the result of falling from a height. The ground cover is an important consideration, as well. Sand, pea gravel, or small or shredded wood chips to a depth of at least 15 cm (6 inches) will soften the impact of a fall. Grass is soft too, but it can get worn down quickly and the ground beneath it can become concrete hard in a short time. The ground cover should extend out from the play area for about 1.8 m (6 feet) in all directions.

❋

Avoid installing equipment that has V-shaped openings or openings that are between 10 cm (4 inches) and 17 cm (7 inches) in diameter. Kids want to get their heads in the darndest places!

❋

Designate a section of the garden as the play area so it's clear what is off limits. If the children also have a place where they can plant and nurture some of their own things, such as sunflowers or scarlet runner beans, they will learn to respect the plantings of others. If you haven't got the space to do this and want to give the entire garden over to the children, fulfil your gardening needs by planting in containers or putting all your energy into the front garden. The years we have with our small children are really very short and the time to garden when they have grown is quite long.

## PLAY AREA EQUIPMENT

❋

Swings and sandboxes are the mainstays of any play area. These two simple pieces of play equipment can provide kids with many happy hours. Provide your sandbox with a cover that is put on when the box isn't in use to keep out cats and other animals. When the sandbox has outgrown its usefulness, turn it into a flower bed or water garden.

Kids love tree houses — it's a great place to get away from parents. They enjoy being higher than you! Have you ever been in the wonderful tree house at Disney World? It brings out the kid in all of us. Allow kids to try designing the house themselves — who knows, it may be all the start they need to be future garden designers! A tree house doesn't have to be elaborate: a good sturdy platform with equally sturdy walls and a ladder will do. Be careful how you attach the structure to the tree. Nails are fine, especially if the tree house will not be a permanent addition to your garden. If you want it to stay put for more than four or five years, large screws can be used. Lashing the tree house to the tree with cable can cause damage to the tree. Not all trees are suitable to having a house built in them. There must be a horizontal plane on which the platform can be built. If you have two strong

*What's better for a kid than a tree house? The only disadvantage may be that every child in the neighbourhood will be in your back yard!*

trees growing fairly closely together, the tree house could span the two trees. As well, a tree house could be built on well-grounded stilts, either with the tree coming up the middle of the platform or to one side of the platform. Access to tree houses is provided by a ladder (preferably not hammered to the tree) or a rope ladder that can be pulled up after the last person is in.

# LIGHTING

Extend the pleasure your garden gives by adding some lighting. Temporary lighting such as that provided by candles, lamps, flares, and torches can whet your appetite for more permanent installations.

Lighting performs several functions in the garden:

❁ Security: A well-lit garden and front entrance discourage strangers from entering your property.

❁ Safety: Light paths and steps so that guests can walk safely.

*Coach lamp*

*Low level accent light*

*Raised spotlight*

*Taller accent light*

*Post light*

✳ Aesthetics: Highlight a feature of the garden — a tree, shrub, or statue.

✳ Keeping bugs away: Some lights are designed to keep bugs away.

## TYPES OF LIGHTS

✳ Accent lights, low-voltage fixtures, are perfect for use along walkways. They are usually designed with a cap and louvres that are adjustable or removable so you can direct the light where you want it. They are easy to install and available in many garden centres and hardware stores. The transformer that plugs into the outlet sometimes contains a timer that you can set so your lights turn on and off at a particular time. A solenoid switch activates with the setting and rising of the sun.

✳ Floodlights are used to light a particular feature, create a mood, or provide security lighting. Some have a variable focus ring to help customize the light you want. Others feature a motion-detector so that they come on only when they sense movement.

✳ Post lights and garden lights are taller than accent lights but they too have adjustable louvres. They throw out a wider beam of light and are used for pathways or in flower beds.

## LIGHTING TIPS

✳ Use restraint when you are installing light in the garden. More is not necessarily better. Keep it simple for maximum effect. A well-directed spotlight will have greater impact than a floodlight lighting the whole garden.

✳ Light plants from below rather than from overhead for a dramatic effect.

❄ Lights used to illuminate a path should be above or below eye level to avoid blinding people walking.

❄ Use our long winter to advantage. Light stark branches to cast shadows on the snow for a spectacular effect. In a snow fall, the light will catch the falling flakes, creating a constantly changing garden feature.

❄ Use garden plantings and structures to conceal the lighting fixtures, unless the fixtures themselves are ornamental.

❄ Avoid aiming a floodlight into an area where you will be sitting and by all means avoid flooding your neighbours' yard with light, depriving them of their privacy!

❄ Use a small spotlight to direct the light at the object when lighting statuary, an interesting wall, or a particular plant. Experiment to get the best play of light and shadow.

❄ Use lighting to emphasize shrubs and trees with interesting leaves and branches, such as the corkscrew hazel.

❄ A light that shines down through branches and leaves gives a dappled (and sometimes spooky!) effect.

❄ Hire an electrician to install permanent electrical lighting and power supplies throughout the garden. This is not a job for an amateur. Electrical outlets need three-pronged outlets and should be grounded; they should be equipped with a cover. Note carefully the placement of buried cables so you won't inadvertently slice through one as you dig a new bed.

❄ Look for the CSA label and be sure it's meant for outdoor use when purchasing light bulbs, extension cords, or any electrical equipment.

❄ Look for solar-powered lights if you don't want to use electric lighting. The range available is not as wide, but they are not hard to find.

*Lighting a garden at night can be especially beautiful in the winter.*

❀ Use motion-activated floodlights for security.

❀ Add mystery and excitement to a water garden with an underwater light, especially if it catches the glint of goldfish moving in the water. And don't forget the swimming pool — it can look extraordinarily beautiful when lit at night from underwater.

❀ Light a fountain so that the light goes through the jet of water, creating sparkling jewels of water.

## FENCES, WALLS, HEDGES, WALKWAYS, PATHS, AND GATES

It seems to me that until recently Canadians have been reluctant to use fences, walls, and hedges to clearly define the boundaries of their property. Perhaps it's an attitude left over from the days when our ancestors came to this land and revelled in the wide open spaces — who could possibly want to contain it? Somehow fences in those days seemed downright un-neighbourly!

Fences, walls, and hedges all have their place in modern gardens and they don't have to be unneighbourly or unfriendly at all. In the stress and hurly-burly of life today, we all want a place to relax in, unwind, and relish the world of nature in our garden. It doesn't matter if it's a balcony, a small patio, or an acre in the country, it can provide the same healing properties. Fences, walls, and hedges provide the privacy necessary to create such a sanctuary. They can also be used as architectural details to make outdoor rooms of our garden. They help to define space, which is one of the fundamentals of garden design.

Gates and paths are the features that draw us further into the garden, inviting us to explore as they lead us along. There is nothing as enticing as a partially opened gate and a path that curves gently, inviting you to just tiptoe in to see what lies around the corner.

## Fences and Walls

A wall makes a much bolder statement than a fence, but both can be incorporated into the landscape in a way that is quite natural. The uses of fences and walls are almost endless and many a suburban garden can be made spectacular with the addition of a waist-high fence or wall. It does not have to be around the perimeter, but can be used as a design feature to separate two parts of the garden, or to provide a backdrop for a cherished plant or ornament.

Some construction materials are more appropriate for walls than for fences — for example, a construction of brick seems to me to deserve to be called a wall, whereas one of wood or wrought iron is a fence. Walls and fences serve many of the same purposes, and so I am discussing them together.

When choosing the material and style for fences and walls, remember the feel of your garden. A rustic rail fence is appropriate in a cottage garden, a wrought iron fence looks better in a more formal garden.

A few practical considerations:

❋  Before building any fence, check with your municipality about height restrictions.

❋  There are sometimes specifications for the amount of airflow that passes between fences, so if you want to install a solid fence, be sure you're not breaking a bylaw.

❋  If you are sharing the cost of a fence with your neighbour (and therefore agree on the design, materials, and so forth), the fence can be built right on the property line; if you can't agree with your neighbour on the style and cost of the fence and want to go it alone, check to see if you local bylaw allows you to put it 2.5 cm (1 inch) inside your side of the property line.

❋  A good-neighbour wooden fence is the type where a base stringer runs the length of the boundary and the planks are nailed to each side alternately. This results in a fence where there is no right or wrong or good or bad side — both sides look exactly the same. However, if you end up on the "wrong" side of a new fence, use it to your advantage: grow vines over it, attach pots to it, cover sections in lattice, attach shelves to it ... you get the idea.

❋  Higher isn't always better. A tall fence or wall

*A good-neighbour fence has neither a right side nor a wrong side.*

around a small area can make the garden seem somewhat claustrophobic. Clever plantings will help to soften the impact of the boxed-in feeling.

Some fences mark boundaries and carry through the theme of the garden but don't provide concealment. Picket fences and wrought iron fences are two examples.

Chain link fencing, in my books, is just about the least attractive fencing around but it is inexpensive, easy to install, and relatively long lasting. Disguise chain link fencing with some climbing plants — if one of them is evergreen, so much the better. Unadorned chain link looks no more attractive in winter than in summer. You can also attach sheets of bamboo reeds to chain link fencing. This type of cover-up will have to be replaced every few years, but it is inexpensive, attractive, easy to install, and gives an interesting texture.

Wooden fences are also easy to install and most home do-it-yourselfers can easily install one. Another advantage is that wooden fences can be designed to fit into nearly every garden design from Japanese gardens to wildflower gardens to formal rose gardens. Wooden fences should be treated with a preservative (not creosote, which can damage plants) or painted. In order to prevent rotting, the palings (planks) should not touch the ground. The tops of the palings can be finished with a decorative cut or left square or rounded.

Fences requiring painting or staining are best kept free of vines and other climbers but need to be set off and softened by plantings in front.

Building supply centres carry ready-made fencing sold by the panel — a quick and easy way to install a fence. Lattice panels are a pretty way to hide an unsightly view. They provide privacy, allow air movement, act as a trellis, finish off the gap between a deck and the ground ... it's not hard to see why this is such a popular solution.

If a wall is an extension of the house, it should be constructed of the same material as the house. Such walls often make little "suntraps" — places that warm up quickly in the spring and stay warm well into the fall, making nice corners for a little table and chair, a place to sit and catch a few rays. A pot of daffodils and crocuses in the spring or chrysanthemums in the fall adds to the ambience of a suntrap.

Low walls can be used to separate parts of a garden, to break up a large open space, to provide seating, or to surround a patio.

Walls can be constructed of stone, concrete or concrete block, brick, or railway ties.

It may seem odd, but once we get a wall built, we want to cover it up — it's like a blank canvas waiting for the artist to get started. Good plant "paints" for blank walls include such climbers as bittersweet, clematis, climbing hydrangea, silver lace vine, wisteria, trumpet vine, Boston ivy, and English ivy. Not all these will cling to the wall. Some plants may need supports to twine themselves around.

*The rapid growth and lovely flowers of the clematis make it perfect to cover or hide a blank wall or fence.*

## HEDGES

Hedges perform the same function as walls and fences — to enclose, protect, offer privacy, provide shelter, hide an unattractive view, define spaces, and so forth. They can be free-flowing and informal or, when clipped closely, a formal backdrop for showing off specimen plants, figurines or sculptures, or furniture.

The plants that make up a hedge can be planted in a straight row, in a curve, or go around corners. The hedge can be tall or short, it can have openings clipped into it, it can have a scalloped top, it can be combined with walls, fences, and gates to fill in where a separation is desired but where a wall or fence isn't appropriate or easy to install — on a hillside, for example.

Some plants that make good hedges in most parts of Canada: European beech — a deciduous plant that holds onto some of its brown leaves into the winter; boxwood — makes a beautiful slow-growing thick evergreen hedge that may need some winter protection in very cold areas; cypress — evergreen, quick growing, resulting in more frequent clipping; yew — makes a dense evergreen hedge and is relatively slow growing, resulting in infrequent clipping; hawthorn — deciduous, its thorns act as an effective animal control; caragana — another deciduous plant that's a good choice for dry regions such as the prairies. eastern white cedar — evergreen, can be grown in sun or shade, probably the most commonly used hedging plant in Canada.

Plant hedges in a single row or double staggered rows. The double staggered row produces a strong, dense hedge and will seem to fill in more quickly.

In a large garden, a hedged corridor can direct the eye to a piece of sculpture or specimen plant situated at its end. A hedge makes the perfect enclosure for a "secret garden" — a place not visible from any other part of the garden.

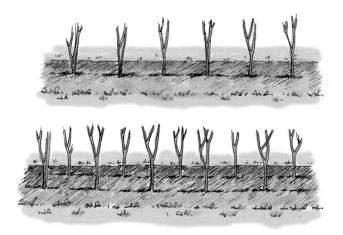

*A hedge can be planted in one row, top, or in parallel rows where the plants are staggered, bottom. The double staggered rows produce a very dense hedge.*

*Topiary can be fun to incorporate into the garden.*

## RULE OF THUMB:

Make the bottom of the hedge wider than the top when pruning. This will allow light and air to get into the interior.

## TOPIARY

When you clip a hedge in decorative ways, you are undertaking a type of topiary — pruning plants to whimsical or geometric shapes. Most topiary is freestanding, although it can be quite inventive when incorporated in a hedge. Even a couple of box or bay plants in containers are turned into miniature topiary plantings when they have been clipped into square or round shapes on top of their slender stems. More fanciful and intricate shapes, such as animals, spirals, and chess pieces are created by using wire to direct the plant's growth in a fashion similar to bonsai growing. Plants used in topiary have to be kept in extremely good health with regular watering and fertilizing.

## PATHS AND GATES

Part of the charm of many gardens is the sense of mystery, which is brought about by partially concealing its treasures. Paths and gates are instrumental in introducing this sense of intrigue — what could possibly be beyond the gate or around the bend of the path?

Gates, needless to say, have a practical purpose — they keep four-legged and two-legged intruders out. They say, "This is where the private part starts." Paths lead you to the gate and take you beyond it. Of course, paths exist without gates, but most gates are approached by a path.

*A flagstone path bordered with flowers and foliage plants is an inviting entry to the garden.*

## FURNISHINGS

❀ The path directs your steps, taking you someplace, controlling your movement through the garden. The path should have a purpose, so plan its placement carefully and thoughtfully. Give the visitor a reward at the end of a path — a view, a place to sit, a hidden surprise not visible at the outset.

❀ The surface of the path is dictated by the use the path will get. Will it be used for ferrying gardening equipment back and forth between the front and back gardens, for visiting the compost, or for getting visitors to the gazebo or swimming pool? In each case the surface treatment will vary.

❀ A grass path is cool and comfortable to walk on, but will quickly get worn down if it's used frequently.

❀ Some natural paving materials are pea gravel, crushed rock or stone, flagstones, slate, and bark chips. A hard surface is provided by flagstones, slate,

*There are right and wrong ways to build a path. A short path (left) that is needlessly interrupted is rather pointless; a path that winds due to plantings is much better designed.*

brick, and concrete. You don't have to confine your-self to one element, either — mix several types of stone or stone and brick, brick and cement, wooden blocks and bricks, and so on.

Concrete paving stones are available in a wide vari-ety of colours and patterns, some of them doing an extremely good job of mimicking flagstones.

Consider upkeep when planning paths. Stones or concrete pads set into grass will need special atten-tion at mowing time to keep the grass growing at their edges well-clipped.

Good drainage is vital, so the path should be a bit higher than surrounding beds and lawns so they will dry quickly after rain and not collect water.

If children and elderly people will be using the paths, build them of a smooth, non-slip material. The materials should be firmly set with no gaps between sections unless you want to grow specific ground-hugging plants (such as thyme, Irish moss, or grass) between the stones or pavers.

If the path is one that has to be kept clear of snow, a solid surface is preferable so that you are not moving shovelsful of gravel, crushed rock, or bark chips with every toss of the snow shovel.

If you already have a paved driveway, a patio, or a deck, choose materials for your paths that are com-plementary. Take into account the colour and tex-ture and how they fit your overall garden design.

A formal garden usually has paths set out in a symmetri-cal fashion. Informal gardens use curving, free-flowing shapes for paths and borders. However, even a formal layout can be given an informal feeling by allowing plants to creep and spill into the path area.

Unless its purpose is to give total privacy and security, a gate that allows the passerby a glimpse into the garden provides that important sense of allure and mystery.

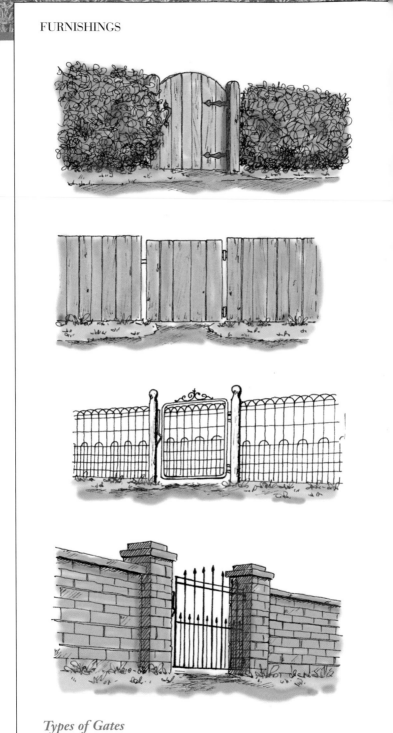

### Types of Gates

*Gates should be an integral part of the fence, and their design should complement the fencing material.*

A gate needs to be well supported by its hinges and support posts, especially if there are children about — there's nothing better than swinging on a gate! A gate should serve its purpose of keeping people (kids?) in or out.

The frame must be well constructed to allow it to close properly. Diagonal cross braces in a wooden gate will ensure that it will not sag.

Decorative hinges and other hardware can add an individual touch to your gate. If you can't find what you want at the hardware store, look for someone who works with wrought iron or other metal. You can also hire a carpenter to build you a gate that you have designed. Many skilled artisans will take on such commissions, and you will have a one-of-a-kind addition to your garden.

# FURNISHING FOR BIRDS

I think Canadian gardeners owe a great deal of thanks to birds. Without them our winter gardens would be quite dull.

Gardens are not only sanctuaries for people and plants, they are sanctuaries for birds and animals, too. Many gardeners plant flowers, trees, and shrubs that produce berries and seeds that are attractive to birds. Bird feeders, nesting boxes, and bird baths are physical structures that can be decorative as well as offering the protection and nourishment birds need. When you are designing your garden, don't forget to include these structures in your plan. In fact, a bird bath could make a focal point in a small garden. On a hot summer day, the eye will be attracted to it naturally, for it will be a centre of great activity. I have seen eight or nine sparrows in a bird bath, making an entertaining sight and sound as they cavort in a few inches of refreshing water, splashing it every which way.

Birds are naturally drawn to gardens, but you can increase the bird populations by providing places for nesting, eating, and drinking. Not only do birds help keep insect populations under con-

*Bird houses bring the life — and activity! — of birds to the garden.*

trol, but they also add life, movement, and interest to a garden.

When you choose the style of bird bath or nesting box, think about the type of garden you have. It's not hard to find bird houses that look like thatched English cottages — an attractive addition to a garden full of roses, hollyhocks, and baby's breath.

## NESTING BOXES (Bird Houses)

Nesting boxes, a more accurate name than bird houses since birds nest rather than live in them, attract birds that build their nests in cavities. They can be simple or decorative structures — what they look like doesn't matter to the bird. Whether you build or buy, make sure the nesting box has drainage holes, a way of attaching it to the tree, and a method of getting into the box to clean it out.

❋ Place nesting boxes at least 1.5 m (5 feet) above the ground where they won't be in direct sunlight or exposed to heavy rain. Try to position the box so that it is visible from the house or your favourite sitting spot in the garden. You will then have the enjoyment of watching the activity of nest building and rearing of the young. Remember that you will have to clean it out, so don't make reaching it a big chore. The box can be attached to a tree, pole, or the wall of an outbuilding such as a shed or garage.

❋ The roof, preferably sloping, should extend over the front of the box by 2.5 cm to 5 cm (1 to 2 inches) to protect the inside from sun and rain. Situate the box so that it is not facing into prevailing winds.

*Types of nesting boxes or bird houses.*

❊

Small birds like small boxes. A floor area of 10 cm x 10 cm (4 x 4 inches) will be just fine for birds such as chickadees, titmice, house wrens, bluebirds, and the downy woodpecker. The tree swallow needs a slightly larger floor area, 12.5 cm x 12.5 cm (5 x 5 inches), and the northern flicker, a larger bird, needs a space 17 cm x 17 cm (7 x 7 inches).

❊

The size of the entrance hole varies according to the bird as well. It should be just large enough to allow the bird to enter but not large enough to admit a predator or larger bird. An "all-purpose" hole should be just under 4 cm (1–1/2 inches) in diameter; a hole larger than this would allow starlings to get in. The downy woodpecker makes the smallest hole when constructing its own nesting spot — just over 3 cm (1–1/4 inches) in diameter. Larger birds, such as flickers, will need a correspondingly larger hole but be prepared for starling invasions.

❊

The entrance hole should be placed high enough that when the bird builds the nest, the edge of the nest will be below the hole. Leave a depth of 5 cm to 7.5 cm (1 to 2 inches) for the nest, then a space of 7.5 cm to 10 cm (3 to 4 inches) from the top of the nest to the hole. The space between the hole and lip of the nest is important as it makes it difficult for a predator to reach. It also prevents the young birds from falling out of the box, while still allowing them to put their heads out as they wait for their parents to bring food. Robins, however, prefer a box that is fairly open at the front. A protective piece of wood or other material can cover the lower half, but the top half should be open.

❊

Wood is the best material for a nesting box. It has insulating properties that protect the inhabitants from extremes of heat or cold. Purple martin houses are often made of aluminum, and this is the one case where metal makes an acceptable house.

*A dovecote can add a totally romantic touch to the garden.*

❀ Decorate or paint the box, if you wish. In fact, here's where you can be really creative and match the house to the formality or informality of your garden. Be cautious about paints and stains you use. Lead-based paints, creosote, and pressure-treated lumber can be harmful to birds.

❀ If a purchased nesting box is lacking a perch, there's no need for concern. A perch is not necessary for birds that nest in cavities.

❀ Late winter or early spring is the best time to put up nesting boxes so that they are ready for birds returning from their wintering spots.

❀ Some gardeners want to attract bats because of their great insect-eating capabilities. Bat boxes are simple to make — a four-sided slim box, with a top and open bottom and the rough side of the wood on the inside. The bat enters the bottom and hangs upside down inside.

❀ For a totally romantic touch, why not make a dove-cote the centrepiece of your garden? They are usually made of wood and are topped with a cone-shaped roof, usually shingled but sometimes thatched. They can be as elaborate or as simple as you like; some have perches or even small verandahs. They should have large openings for the pigeons or doves. Many are round or octagonal, although some are flat on one side so they can be attached to a wall.

## BIRD BATHS

Here's where whimsy can really come into play. Just about anything that will hold water — from an overturned garbage can lid to a one-of-a-kind shallow ceramic bowl — can make a bird bath. As with nesting boxes, and everything you put in the garden, try to make the bird bath fit in with the feeling or theme of your garden.

Water in a garden gives a sense of serenity so a bird bath, positioned well, can serve two purposes. It provides a peaceful spot for the eye to rest as the

*A bird bath should be positioned far enough from the house so that birds will not be afraid to use it, yet close enough that you can still enjoy their company.*

bath reflects the blue of the sky, and it supplies the birds — and sometimes squirrels and the neighbourhood cat — with water on warm summer days.

❀ A container with a diameter of about 30 cm (12 inches) and a depth of about 7.5 cm (3 inches) is large enough for a small group of birds to bathe and drink.

❀ A bird bath with several depths will attract a wider variety of birds.

❀ Containers placed on pedestals can be extremely attractive and also provide protection from predators. Some birds, as they do in the wild, prefer to take their water near the ground. Try placing the bird bath on a wide railing, a deck, or even on a path, but be sure there's a bush close by where birds can quickly seek safety. They are also likely to sit in the bush to check the area out before they commit themselves to swooping down to the bird bath.

❀ It can take a while for birds to come to the bird bath, especially if it is near the house. If you can trickle some water nearby, they will be attracted by the sound.

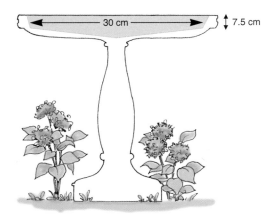

*A bird bath should be about 30 cm (12 inches, minimum) across and at least 7.5 cm (3 inches) deep. Several depths are good to attract a wider variety of birds.*

❀ Plastic birdbaths can be slippery for a bird (they can also tip over easily), so scatter some small pebbles over the bottom of the bowl to make it easier for the birds to gain a foothold.

❀ Most other materials are entirely satisfactory — metal, stone, ceramic — you should be able to find a bird bath to fit any garden decor. Visit a potter's studio or metal worker's shop to see what they offer. I've come across some amusing, beautiful, and unique bird baths that are truly works of art.

❀ If you have a water garden or are planning one, see if you can work into the design a corner that is attractive to birds. Water trickling into a hollowed-out stone set into a corner of the pond will entice birds. Even something as simple as a few flat stones jutting out of the water for birds to stand on will make it easier for them to sip.

❀ Change the water every few days, especially in hot weather when algae will start to bloom.

❀ In winter, use an electric heater specially designed to be used in bird baths to prevent the water from freezing. Birds need water in the winter every bit as much as they do in the summer. Never put antifreeze or any other additive into the water you put out for the birds.

❀ If you don't want to keep your bird bath outside in the winter, empty it and store it in a protected area. Water that freezes and thaws can crack even a stone bird bath.

## BIRD FEEDERS

We seem to have a natural instinct to nurture small creatures, and this is readily apparent when you look in Canadians' back yards. Most of us have at least one bird feeder that we keep well stocked throughout the winter and sometimes into the summer.

Attracting birds to the garden, whether by providing food in feeders or planting shrubs which are appealing to birds, brings life and interest to the garden. This is especially important in the winter. To suddenly see the red flash of a cardinal against the white snow always makes my heart jump. Get the kids involved, too — they'll love to watch chickadees dipping through the air. These friendly and fearless little birds will come nearer the house than most birds, making it easy for kids to watch their antics. If you keep a bird guide near at hand you will be able to work with the kids to identify all the visitors to your garden.

There is a bird feeder for nearly every place in the garden. The problem we all face is trying to prevent the large birds, such as jays, pigeons, and starlings, and those four-footed marauders, squirrels, from gobbling down food not intended for them.

Whether you purchase a bird feeder or construct your own, there are several things to keep in mind.

❋ The feeder should be close enough to the house so that you can see the birds and keep it filled with seed.

❋ The feeder should provide protection for the food so that it doesn't become wet. Suet balls, however, are usually exposed to the weather.

❋ Some birds feed on the ground, some need to have a perch as they eat, others like to cling to something vertical.

❄ A place of safety, such as a tree or shrub, should be near the location of the feeder so the birds don't feel too exposed.

## TYPES OF FEEDERS

Feeders on poles, hanging feeders, feeders that attach to windows — how do you choose the one that's right for you?

❄ Features always to look for: seed is protected from rain and snow; ease of filling; ease of cleaning; good capacity, to cut down on trips to fill feeder (although if you have squirrels around, it will always be empty!).

❄ Hanging or pole-mounted feeders: Many hanging or pole-mounted feeders are of the hopper type — that is, they dispense seed as it is used. The advantage is that the seed-holding compartment needs filling less frequently than a feeder in which the seed is set out such as in an open box or platform. Hanging feeders usually dispense a specific type of seed, such as sunflower seeds or niger thistle seed, although some will take mixed seeds. Sunflower seed is the most popular choice for attracting a variety of birds — chickadees, goldfinches, sparrows, jays, woodpeckers, nuthatches, cardinals, and more.

❄ Window feeders: A suction cup attaches these clear plastic feeders to the window. The seed-holding compartment is usually smaller than in other feeders, so more frequent filling is necessary. If there are kids in your house, this is a great type of feeder because the birds come so close to the house to feed. Window feeders can also be as simple as a piece of shelving attached to the window sill, but if it is too exposed to the elements, the food will get wet or will blow away.

❀ Ground tables or platforms: It is possible to scatter seed on the ground for birds that prefer to take their food that way, but you can also use a table or sheet of wood if you want to keep the seed off the ground as much as possible. Ground-feeding birds are often attracted by the seed that falls from pole-mounted or hanging feeders. Some birds that eat from the ground are juncos, mourning doves, jays, sparrows, blackbirds, and cardinals.

❀ Suet feeders: Suet feeders are small "cages" either purchased at a store or made from household items such as onion bags. Suet, a high-energy food for birds, is available from butchers or can be bought in cakes at birders' stores or garden centres. Suet can melt and go rancid in hot weather, so it is best to confine its use to the colder months. If you buy suet from the butcher, you can make special treats for the birds by heating the suet and mixing in peanuts,

*A pole mounted feeder and a ground table or platform feeder. Each attracts specific types of birds.*

seeds, raisins, currants, and peanut butter. Pack it in onion bags and hang in a tree. Suet can also be stuffed into holes drilled into logs, or pine cones can be rolled in the suet mixture and hung outside.

Wooden or plastic bird feeders are better as metal ones can have sharp edges and rusty spots. Pole-mounted wooden feeders will be more stable than plastic ones, but hanging plastic feeders are extremely good.

## PROBLEMS AT THE FEEDER

There is nothing more frustrating than filling a feeder on a bitterly cold winter morning then seeing the contents gobbled up by a squirrel almost before you are back in the house. There is only so far you can go in manipulating nature, though. Cats will always stalk birds, but you can outsmart some predators and unwanted birds to a certain extent.

Put a bell on the cat — although cats can eventually learn how to stalk in such a manner that the bell stays silent! Keep the feeder or bird bath away from extremely dense ground foliage, a perfect place for the cat to hide. Did you know that cats are one of the reasons for the decline in songbirds in Canada?

Pole-mounted feeders are the main target of squirrels. Squirrels seem able to climb up the thinnest and the slipperiest poles. Fortunately, many types of squirrel baffles are available to fit on poles, some of them more successful than others. Squirrels can jump great distances, so even if you have thwarted them by using baffles, they can still reach feeders by propelling themselves from fences, walls, trees, and any other object they can climb. Situate poles at least 2.5 m (8 feet) from the nearest squirrel take-off point and the feeder itself should be 150 cm to 180 cm (5 to 6 feet) from the ground. The baffle should be about 120 cm (4 feet) from the ground. If you are making your own baffle, its diameter should be at least six times the diameter of the pole on which it will be mounted. Make baffles that hang over the feeder 5 cm (2 inches) in diameter larger than the largest dimension of the feeder. Some bird feeders are constructed in such a way that if anything too heavy — like a squirrel — sits on the perch, the door slams shut.

❋ Try mixing some cayenne pepper into the bird seed. The taste buds of birds are not as sensitive as squirrels' so the birds won't mind but the squirrels will.

❋ Supply the squirrels with cracked corn on the ground. This will help to divert their attention from the feeder.

❋ There is no way of preventing squirrels from feeding at ground tables or platforms so accept the fact that you are feeding them as well as the birds — and enjoy their antics.

❋ If you feel that large or undesirable birds are hogging all the food, buy mixtures and bird feeders designed only for small birds. Many cylindrical hanging feeders are difficult for large birds to feed from — and they are virtually squirrel-proof, as well.

## ATTRACTING BIRDS

Birds, like humans, have their favourite food. To attract particular birds to your garden, give them the food they like. Do some research to see which birds winter in your area — no matter what you put out, you are unlikely to attract a ring-necked pheasant in the heart of Montreal or tufted titmice unless you live at the very southern tip of Canada.

*One of the sure signs of spring is when robins come back to the garden.*

❀ **SUNFLOWER SEEDS:** An all-purpose seed that attracts chickadees, cardinals, common flicker, blue jays, sparrows, purple finches, pine siskins, grackles, nuthatches, and tufted titmice.

❀ **CORN:** Whole, crushed, or milled attracts cardinals, cowbirds, crows, doves, ducks, flickers, Canada geese, grackles, red-breasted and evening grosbeaks, ruffed grouse, slate-coloured juncos, sparrows, hairy woodpeckers.

❀ **MILLET:** Very fine seed. Scatter on ground to attract cardinals, mallard ducks, mourning doves, purple and gold finches, Canada geese, slate-coloured juncos, pigeons, redpolls, and sparrows.

❀ **OATS:** Use in seed, crushed, or rolled. Attracts blackbirds, cardinals, rock doves, grackles, grosbeaks, slate-coloured juncos, ring-necked pheasants, sparrows, and rufous-sided towhees.

❀ **SUET:** A type of hard fat found near beef kidney and

loins. Buy it in cakes at a birders' store or make your own mixes; buy the suet from the butcher and add various nuts and grains to it. Attracts nearly all birds, especially chickadees, nuthatches, starlings, and woodpeckers.

❄ Peanuts: Shelled peanuts attract blackbirds, cardinals, catbirds, chickadees, crows, purple finches, slate-coloured juncos, nuthatches, pigeons, robins, sparrows, tufted titmice, some woodpeckers, and wrens.

❄ Coconuts: Split a coconut in half and hang it outside. Attracts chickadees.

❄ Raisins and currants: May attract bluebirds.

**HUMMINGBIRDS** The ruby-throated hummingbird is the only hummingbird that visits Canada, so seeing one makes the experience all the more special. You will find it in the Maritimes and along the southern part of Canada but not in B.C. If you can attract them to your garden, you can have hours of fun watching them zoom about and twittering at one another.

Their favourite colour is red, so planting red flowers is a good start. You can also buy or make a feeder and fill it with purchased or homemade sugar water. Mix one part of sugar to four parts of water. Boiling the mixture and letting it cool or using distilled water prevents it from fermenting, but don't add any red colouring to the sugar water as it could be harmful to the hummingbird.

## FEEDER CARE

Feeders should be cleaned at the end of the season, or throughout the year if you feed the birds

*Hummingbirds like red flowers—the reason for the colour and shape of this feeding tube.*

all year round. Scrub feeders with hot water and detergent and rinse well. Let them dry thoroughly before restocking. Discard old or mouldy food.

Don't use paints or stains on wooden bird feeders for fear of contaminating the food.

## PLANTING FOR BIRDS

The seeds and other food you provide birds should be seen as an augmentation to the food Mother Nature provides. Leave the seed heads on your annual and perennial plants over winter to provide food for the birds. Here are some planting suggestions that will attract birds to your garden.

* Conifers: The cone seeds of trees such as fir, spruce, larch, and hemlock, attract chickadees, juncos, jays, finches, grosbeaks, and nuthatches.

* White Birch: The redpolls, pine siskins, and goldfinch love the seed of this popular tree.

❋ Mountain Ash: This ornamental tree has brilliantly coloured berries which are enjoyed by robins, cedar waxwings and other birds, but they do not seem to like the berries from the Leonard Springer variety of Mountain Ash.

❋ Serviceberries: The small fruits are eaten by woodpeckers, cedar waxwings, northern orioles, grosbeaks, cardinals, finches, blue jays, and chickadees.

❋ Raspberries, blackberries: The fruit from these and other small fruit bushes will attract a variety of birds.

❋ Asters: Their seeds attract seed-eating birds such as cardinals, finches, sparrows, titmice, and chickadees.

❋ Dogwoods: Dogwoods produce berries that are eaten by more than 98 species of bird, including flickers, tanagers, downy woodpeckers, cardinals, robins, bluebirds, cedar waxwings, and thrushes.

*Sunflowers can be harvested for their seeds, which chickadees, goldfinches and sparrows, among others, enjoy.*

❋
Sunflowers: Grow your own seeds to attract mourning doves, blackbirds, chickadees, house finches, goldfinches, sparrows, and titmice.

❋
Hollies: Hollies provide food, nesting sites, and shelter for flickers, bluebirds, cedar waxwings, robins, and many other birds.

❋
Columbines, rhododendrons, azaleas, bleeding heart, petunias, snapdragon, and trumpet vines and most flowers that are red in colour and tubular in shape attract hummingbirds in the summer.

❋
Virginia Creeper: This climbing vine with its shiny black berries will attract kingbirds, flycatchers, and bluebirds.

# ❀ NOTES: ❀

..................................................................................

..................................................................................

..................................................................................

..................................................................................

..................................................................................

..................................................................................

..................................................................................

..................................................................................

..................................................................................

..................................................................................

..................................................................................

..................................................................................

..................................................................................

..................................................................................

..................................................................................

..................................................................................

..................................................................................

..................................................................................

# INDEX

# See all 4 volumes in *The Complete Gardener* series:

**MARK CULLEN**
THE COMPLETE GARDENER

**COLOUR & DESIGN**

Simplifies the process of design and demystifies the issue of colour. Essential information for planning your garden so it looks its best. Includes planting instructions on making your own all-white garden regardless of your garden size. Accompanied by video.

**MARK CULLEN**
THE COMPLETE GARDENER

**FURNISHINGS**

Learn how to add interest and charm through the furnishings in your garden. From arbours to urns—they're here! Features step-by-step directions for making and planting a "stone" trough that would cost a small fortune to buy! Accompanied by video.

**MARK CULLEN**
THE COMPLETE GARDENER

**PLANTING & GROWING**

These fundamentals of good gardening practice will help you to create and keep a garden full of blooming, healthy plants. Don't miss the recipe for compost tea—your plants will love it! Accompanied by video.

**MARK CULLEN**
THE COMPLETE GARDENER

**PLANTS**

Helps you select the best annuals, perennials, vines, ground covers, trees and shrubs and bulbs for your growing conditions. Special instructions on how to plant a beautiful four-season window box. Accompanied by video.

Canada
am